COMPASS LIGHT

Compass Light

HILARY DAVIES

RENARD PRESS

RENARD PRESS LTD

124 City Road
London EC1V 2NX
United Kingdom
info@renardpress.com
020 8050 2928

www.renardpress.com

Compass Light first published by Renard Press Ltd in 2025

Cover design by Will Dady

Printed and bound in the UK on carbon-balanced papers by CMP Books

ISBN: 978-1-80447-159-3

9 8 7 6 5 4 3 2 1

CLIMATE POSITIVE Renard Press is proud to be a climate positive publisher, removing more carbon from the air than we emit and planting a small forest. For more information see renardpress.com/eco.

Contents

COMPASS LIGHT

For JRP

THE VINE, THE ROSEMARY AND THE OLIVE TREE

The Vine, the Rosemary and the Olive Tree

I stepped into dawn:
Heaven was cold,
And clear as water.
On the little terrace with so poor a purchase
– Just a bench and some scuffed dust –
The boom of the sun opened.
The light lit up the vine,
The rosemary and the olive tree;
Red, white, gold filled them.
On a chill soil,
On a spur of northerly ocean,
Their roots have reached in.
They spice the crevices;
They pass crowns one to another
In the crisp air.

I put my hand into the light of the past
And it is there –
That feathered hunter
Who glides in the lane
Down the line of worlds.

Kyparissía

The tyres rubble over the rough road.
We know every dip and catch now in our bodies,
The rattle, the bumps to our bottom
On that little stretch where the goats run down
And the lone tree leans,
Under which we found two hikers once,
Seeking the lost waterfall.
We're away: through the market
And right at the bus station,
Where the swifts swoop in and out
Of the unfinished houses.
What a hurtle down the knotted rows
Of olive trees like honeycombs, past the bluffs
With their beehives looking out to sea.

Kyparissía! Dusty eucalyptus and lemon blossom,
The little cement tiles of the pavements;
On the corner the ironmonger
Who stacks his hardware against three-litre amphorae of wine.
And the barrows of apricots, oranges, peaches!
There is the florist with her improbably large bouquets
Garnished round and round with squeaky cellophane protesting,
And all by her own rose-petalled insignia
Triumphed with love.
Upstream, watch out for the swish of the icy waterfall

From the fishmonger's hosepipe, dazzling his treasures
– Lapis lazuli, purple, silver, rose –
Was there a better display ever in Byzantium?

We're off to Yannis to pay our taxes.
Poor Yannis! That sepia shot of him in the 80s,
All sun-striped T-shirt and delicious smile –
We can't find him these days behind the towering box files,
Bully-belly-rolled by ten thousand souvlakis,
Listening morosely to his worry beads' click-clack.
There's Dimitri, the philosopher, already lodged
In his favourite seat overlooking the square.
He sees everything and is moved by nothing
But disdain for the brouhaha and the dirty demotic.
How would he survive without spleen's pleasures?
What does he see through the veil of himself?

Bah! Bah! It's the 12.20 from Pyrgos,
1950s chrome yellow and blue, stained orange from the Sahara.
It disgorges nine or ten startled tourists condescendingly
On to a sleeping platform.
Did no one tell them it's faster to hitch-hike?
Up in the cottage hospital the friendly doctors
Sit gossiping and smoking; just knock on their door
And they're delighted to help you: numbered tickets
Are no substitute for real presence; we believe
In the personal touch.
Everything here in Kyparissía believes
In the touch of the personal.
That's how we do things – what else is real?

The hands pass hand to hand, back and forth,
On and across, in the setting down of coffee cups
In front of the customers, in the way-pointing
At corners, in the squaring of bricks.
Down by the quayside, a tiny chapel has grown overnight,
All globes and circles, limewash and snow-blue;
She lights the sea-goblets of the fishermen,
Who are never off guard, and the golden wine-drinkers,
Whose guard is elsewhere. The waters sparkle.
Happiness spreads across the white tablecloths.
Fair are the seastars in Kyparissía,
And the bright bread.

At the Bus Station, Kopanaki

The ticket man behind the counter
Finishes serving his usual customers and approaches.
Our transaction is brief but courteous.
Carefully he detaches the green and beige token of passage.
An hour to wait.
I sit outside, like the other travellers,
On the uniquely uncomfortable raffia chairs.
Mine is unstable and rocks me slightly.
It turns me into a blazing south-facing wall
That's still unplastered. Breeze blocks
Quickly and unlovingly slotted one to another –
The cement dripped in places
And has formed little unintentional ornamentations:
Here pearls, there a smudge suggesting a fishtail.
The windows are dark eyes open to the air.

A family gathers farther down: Grandma
Brings from her store container after plastic container
Of sweetmeats and succulences: her son is going far.
The grandchildren stare up at their uncle,
A little frightened, for the first time sensing a threshold.

Pe–eetch! Pe—eetch! Pe——eetch! Threads in the sky,
Steely as needles, fine as silkworms' work;
Dozens, flashing upward to the lip of heaven
And then as wide as the two horizons –

Spooling and streaking
High, high, into the sun's eye,
A swoop, skirr, skim
And wing-dive on their own wind
Down the reams of day to within a nail's breadth of earth
To settle and chatter on a little ledge of summer.

Sweet swifts, fleet and fleeting
– *What seas, what seas* –
Bring us the scent of forest in your feathers,
The four winds' sleet and heat
In your tiny bodies, a planet's turn
In the tilt of your wings.

By the unfinished house
The men are playing heads and tails out of boredom,
A coin's spin, a dream, and the travellers sit
With their knees drawn up, watching,
Half-listening for the sound of the bus
And the worlds it will bear away.

The Gorge

A gash of green on a dry mountainside,
Shivers of silver off the olive trees,
The dark, miraculous, unwonted water.
The land hangs round it, holds its breath,
For the sun is entering his ferocity.
We have pulled our picnic in under the rock:
A ruffled rug, eggshells and crumbs of yolk,
Juice, surplus peaches. Your daughter
And her friend slip their long limbs
In and out of the water,
They lie in a pool of silence,
The dark, miraculous, cooling water.
It is the hour between leaftip and leaftip,
The drenched light dancing.
It is the insects' high festival
In the drowsing air.

The girls yawn and stretch.
'We're going for a walk,' they say.
Yes, to share things that are secret
In that time outside time,
The time we recall without ever being sure
When we entered or when it ended.
But we can see them go into the glades,
Cool-hot, fair, dark, in their bikinis.

Only one returned.
The other had gone walking
Into the kingdom of the olive groves,
Believing it empty.
In that instant, the trees' eyes opened,
And all the branches rustled their ears.
Out of a white blaze, the sun rose,
Watching.
A cave gaped up in the hillside
And I heard the sudden ruttle of goats
Jostling out at its mouth.

Nearer, much nearer, at hand,
Behind the jumble of rocks there,
A hoof struck the earth with deliberation.
A wind passed, but there was no wind
– A glimpse of oiled shoulders through the grey-green glades,
That strange scent in the air –
The trees' trunks turned as if towards some song,
Like bird quiver in the undergrowth,
A rush of presence, a drumming
Which spreads at noon.

The gorge held the sun fast,
While fear's door stood open
And you went searching.
The little stream seemed louder than before,
Its mosses glowed like gems,
Its damselflies flickered a darker, paradise blue.

Then suddenly that dazzle broke away
And rolled over the horizon.
The trees abated.
You brought her back, immaculate.
I saw the fair limbs
Of your daughter and her friend
As the shade fell upon them,
And how their arms shivered.
There was a kind of roar, far off.
The gorge attended.
The river runs, the river runs
Down through the rocks
Where water, dark, miraculous, assuages,
And the deep shadows of the pools
Descend and descend.

Under the Anvil Mountain

Late morning: in under the towering stones,
Through the gateway that swings wide the valley,
A great plain running down to the sea.
The earth glints everywhere scatters of knucklebones
Amongst the orchards; under the olive trees we perch
On a perfect roll of cut stone:
City of glimmering seats, rubbed smooth
By the countless backsides of elders,
Polished by their ceaseless disputations.
Where do these deep watercress beds meander from,
Criss-crossing the carved and derelict gutters?
Frogs deafen in a wet conch of marble.
In the café with the stupendous views
The men are sipping beer and dissecting yesterday's election.
Opposite blazes the pure fountain
Where soldiers filled their billycans
And women their pails. I saw once two mules
Turn their heads towards it as towards heaven.
But we are going farther, up on to the anvil mountain,
From where, they say, you can see the land of milk and honey.

*   *   *

Scrub oak. No one mentions it.
The villagers because it is self-evident.
Tourists because they never encounter it
In condominium or lido. Walkers are madmen.
This is the kingdom of scrub oak,
Which alone knows how to make home
On the broken terraces, where man so wearied
Of clearing the stones away that he now lies under them.
Bushes no higher than a fox's reach
And dense as a garment of thorns,
Just here and there a patch where the sun
Has driven his gimlet in.
When shall we arrive at the sanctuary?
A drink. A rest.
The vision's haze.

Now, just beside my ear,
The minutest crackle, maybe not even a twig,
More the sigh of a dry leaf sinking to ash
And a dry claw foot inching out of the brushwood.
He is no larger than the palm of my hand,
Tiny, gentle creature with his intent eye;
Little tortoise, hanging on the world's hillside,
As am I.
This is steep ground, blue beneath
And blue above,
No telling if our fall is upward
Or into that blue vast below,
Blue a birdwheel and a vertigo,
The tent of the mountain
Stretched on a rim of silence.

*   *   *

In the end there is no need to reach the sanctuary.
The tortoise illuminates the sun.
Look! A cloud passes.
The bees grow louder
And the countryside below
Has unfolded like a fan:
Cypresses' dark cylinders, eucalyptus sway,
The crumpled accidents of rock and bay,
Red fleck of roof, car screens' sudden flash,
A thousand, different, distant noises:
Dog bark, donkey bray, a man building his house
Out of the marble of a buried city
And into his garden calling his friends
To eat the rosemaried lamb
And drink the day.
The water they have brought with them is bliss.
He has planted the blue vine
At last after a lifetime
Amidst all he loves
Under the anvil mountain.

Chasms

Chasm. A gaping fissure. Cleft.
A yawning hollow in a cosmic body.
A void. A separation, striking break
In shape or continuity.
Greek word. Learned word. Poetic word.
Largely figurative in English.
An argument's metaphor.
A rabblerouser's furbelow.
To be avoided, mostly.

*   *   *

Into Arcadia,
A lover's journey.
It was all there in my mind:
The rolling pastoral, bird-hung groves
With their soft horizons, shepherds deciphering
The enigma on the empty tomb.

The road got steeper, suddenly.
Nets had been strung from the cliff in places
To catch falling boulders.
The tarmac had shredded into gravel
And prodigious potholes. No safety barriers.
Violet shadows fell from the crags above.
The bends got sharper.

I noticed how the edge of the road
Slipped away off downwards
In a dark discontinuity
Into which I did not care to look.
And now came a sound below me
Odd in its placement and velocity,
A droning moving too fast to be car or lorry.
Just one peep –
Against the torn scree, a black knot flew
In the deep far down
– Our car crept onwards in the sky above –
A biplane like a gnat
Whose wings glinted as it banked
Round a bluff in the ravine and disappeared.

You touch my arm.
Soon, you say, we will be at the little town
Where once in winter – the snow was falling –
The villagers rushed out, waving 'No! No!'
And how you have never forgotten
The kindness of the people of Stemnitsa
Who gave you hot drinks and bundled you back
Down the rash road you had come.

But now it is spring and this is the way
You want to bring me, as lovers do
Who want more than anything in the world
To show what is precious
To their darling and have it loved.

We arrive at the exquisite hairpin
And the void opens at our feet.
One step distinguishes us from air.
Arcadía!
Nothing, not even your name,
I imagined of you is true.
You stoop like a falcon upon us;
Like a plummet out of the sun
You drop and seize us.
Your gods are the gods of chasm,
Profounder than all algebra, all axioms.
We can guess why the men from the stoa
Tried here to build straight lines
In heaven's thunderclap.
Across the plain a white plume
Lifts like a pillar from the power stations of Megalopoli.
But in these clefts the donkey prevails:
Theirs are the tracks to the subterranean swallow holes,
The dust on their backs carries a scent of rosemary,
They pick their way meticulously over the abyss
Down to where the wild cyclamen and watercress grow
And the sheep come to drink from the cold streams.

Arcadía, your gift breaks our continuity
Like love, that strange country
Across which we gaze, astonished
At its abrupt arrival, its wild geography.

The Dead of Chorion

The men are arguing up in the café.
They sit under the branching mulberry tree.
Taki brings coffee and sweets
From his desultory tin-shack dispensary
And the voices murmur, punctuate, laugh, shout, plummet –
You can hear them all down the valley.
The playing of cards is serious.
Rathena's teeth are going and it shows
When he turns a good hand
And smiles to himself surreptitiously.
Leonidas is smoking, and thinking.
Behind the grill, the little goddess of the gilt inscriptions
Dips with quill and book in her hand.
'What have you got? A six, an ace?'
'You never have anything!' 'Chancer.'
'Life's what luck deals you.' 'No, no,
It's all in the skill you make of what you've been given.'
'But suppose what's to come
Is better, how will I know?'
Pedro has turned his back on the gaggle:
He's not from round here, was a Communist,
Is only tolerated because he married poor little Maroula,
Just four feet tall, who lost her baby
And then went soft in the head with grief.
Maroula who looked at me with doe's eyes
And held out an apple.

'Do you want a beer, Pedro?'
He waves them away over his shoulder
And scuffles his feet.
Ah, if only his men had won, he would for sure
Have become headman of the village
And been able to do it, line them up here
One by one in a row
And machine gun them all
Deliciously over the café wall.

* * *

I enter the room. Athos, our neighbour,
Is lying in bed but greets me warmly,
His eyes on the ceiling.
He never takes his eyes off the ceiling.
He is like a little doll, singing.
The colours here are beige, brown, black,
A faded pastel blue,
The grey of the blanket covering him.
His wife, Dimitroula, brings honey cake
And pink wine in two plain water glasses.
We smile. And smile again. Athos is singing.
She offers me the cake and I take and eat it;
It flakes in the mouth and is very sweet.
I ask her how is her family:
Ah, one son in Athens, another in Melbourne,
Me and Athos went there, years back,
A very long journey, by plane, off this mountain
Where we both were born.
Athos smiles at the ceiling.

There is nothing here but his bed,
And a formica table with ceramic jug of water.
Outside, beyond the frame of the window,
Rises ridge after ridge of hills,
Pearl-blue, violet, indigo,
Rolling up to the sun and the far snow-flash
On the peaks of Taygetos mountain.
Athos is singing: the clear mornings
When he drove his moped down to Kopanaki,
The scent of the rosemary bushes
Before he opened his barber's shop
To lather up his clients and talk the livelong day away
While the train crept at a donkey's pace
Back and forth through the market and the asphodels.
His fingers, they said, were so delicate
It was like a bird snipping your hair away with its beak.
Dimitroula and I sit quietly on our chairs
And stare out over the mountain.

* * *

That was Saturday. Now it is Tuesday.
There are new voices from Athens
Talking loudly on mobile phones in the café below.
From up here by the church you can see
Taki bring trays of sweet coffee
To the burly men in smart, dark suits.
On time, the bell in the branches rings.
And up the ramp so steep the cement
Is slashed to give donkeys and men a foothold
They carry the decorated coffin.

Athos lies very still amongst the compassionate icons.
He never takes his eyes off their blue ceiling.
Rathena has put on his spectacles specially
The better to be able to chant.
They give him an uncustomary, teacherly air.
His tight black curls are oiled
Like a lord's or a cup-bearer's
Among the files of lilies and faces.
The priest is busying himself with thurible and salver
As scrupulously as with his saucepans in his kitchen.
He is at home. We are all at home.

It's not far to the cemetery;
There's a white-dusted track on the hillside,
Pitted by sheeps' hooves.
Mosaic light falls on us from the cypresses.
Everywhere, marble tiptops with photos,
Square-on, blouses starched, jackets pressed,
Slightly startled expressions.
Back by the stove would be friendlier,
With the honey-coloured wine,
But never mind it.
Rathena's taken off his glasses,
No longer cantor but gravedigger.
With the trowel, expertly – remember
He was a ship's stoker, once – he mixes
The lime and water to a creamy paste
And seals Athos in.

The Quernstone

I saw her behind a bush
– Winter had come and gone –
She was wearing a coarse black woollen dress
That showed fawn, knee-high socks
And her puffy ankles.
The hills rose in a hard cradle around her.
A stone lay there, curved, smooth:
That was no coincidence.
With her she had brought a bowl
And another stone, palm-held.
And from the bowl she poured grain,
A cupful, maybe two,
Placed her small stone on top,
Leant forward and, with a rocking movement,
Crushed her grain against the curved, smooth stone.
Silent, slow, she ground her bread.
The breeze shifted a little
And wisps of hair slipped
From beneath her headscarf
In little grey shoots.
The stone rolled and rolled,
Her wrists turning it slightly in a half-circle,
And back, round and back,
With every so often a lift of her forearm
To brush away the threads from her eyes
And the insects that glistened
On her black breast like tears.

The House on the Hill

Rathena's coming to dinner.
We don't have a stove or oven,
Just two portable rings you close up
With an enamel lid each night.
Preparation goes in stages
– The forethought's the pleasure –
Cook the horta first, dress it with lemon,
Lay out the olives, tomatoes, bread sprinkled with rosemary.
If the fig tree poking her leaves through the window
Doesn't distract us, maybe manage some washing-up in the lull.
All that makes space then on the narrow table
For onions, peppers, aubergine
And three pieces of chicken chosen carefully
To be sure they fit in the pot.
Just a few potatoes boil simultaneously beside it.
Here, pillows will be perfect for making those raffia chairs
Palatable to sit on for a whole evening.
We've got the wine, stashed
Over there by your desk in three-litre canisters
Cushioned by those really practical rubber holders
The ironmonger sells them in.
Now we've half an hour
To sit on the philosopher's stone
You slotted into the foundations
And accompany the sun
As he slips below the mountain.

In an instant, the heat goes out like a firework
And the valley darkens into night.

Rathena's here! A little sheepish
In his work jumper, out at one elbow,
But he had to go up to Platania
To collect the bottle of chiparro he wanted to give us
And on the way back there were three flocks
Scuttling down the road to new pastures.
Let's drink! So that we may never forget,
Drink so our thirst may be slaked for ever.
Look! Look at the glow of the rafters
Disappearing high above our heads into the roof
And the candles trembling on the bright, white walls,
The shutters dancing.

'Do you remember
When you first came here alone
And sat in this ruin with one great beam
You'd carried all the way up from the old threshing floor?
We thought you were mad, off your head.
Only strangers can be this mad.
But day after day, with your stones
And your slop bucket, you were content.
You brought more beams. And we thought,
Only the lonely seers have dreams this mad.
So we came to help you.'
Hearing this, the house shifts on her moorings
In delight, lets fall a little silver shower of dust.

You put on music; what does it matter
There are only three of us, and that Rathena prefers,
Not being in his own home, and shy,
To tap out the rhythms on his thigh
With that chiparro glass and hear the cry
Of the singer singing
Of how we live and die
While you turn and turn
With your arms in the air
Like a dragonfly
And the lights of Dorio are tossed
In a maze against the mountain.

* * *

It's late. Rathena takes his leave.
You slide through the trapdoor into sleep below.
There's that mouse in the cupboard
With her familiar tinkle,
And a table abundant with wine,
The chairs pushed back,
A crumpled dishcloth thrown over the chicken pan,
The evening's silence.
Now, very low,
Beyond the glimmer in the grate
Begins another song,
A voice out of the darkness.

What's not spoken of the soul
Is in it, the life we live in
At the edge of words.
Faces gone appear in a doorway;

We learn late to notice their kindness,
How they look at us,
How they build our house our music,
Far rhythm, dark as winter fruit,
Dark as myrrh,
Dark as buried grain.
Out of the night, out of the shadows
Sifts what we ever made of love,
Sifts, echoes, echoes away over the mountain, echoes
Evcharisto
Evcharisto
Evcharisto

THE WILD GRAVE

The Wild Grave

I lay on your grave in the sunlight.
It was high summer
But the wild trees blew.
The dead – so many belovèds! –
Thronged amongst the meadow flowers.

When I pitch restless
On our marriage bed
Do you turn, shift in dream
And reach your arm around me
As you did long ago?

Do you hold me in the wind
That scatters last year's fruit
Across the grass?

In the Eyrie Room

Grief makes us werewolves –
By day I lean on my neighbour's wall
And delight in her children.
Buses sway me amongst the multitudes.
I have errands. Bills. Legal papers.
My friends send messages and invitations.
The lives of families open like fans.
In my garden the sun rolls round his heaven.

Then dusk comes. Nothing immediate.
An itch for company, a chill, a calling in the bone.
I am restless, leap up and down the stairway;
A whimpering begins. Up in the eyrie room
The roof is like a cage. I burst the skylight open
– What sweet release are the icy night breezes –
Eager into my throat gulps the cold air.
Over the housetops I throw my true shape to the stars.

The Messengers

The men in bowler hats
Lifted you through the door.
They had seen me struggle,
Though midnight had gone,
And the party was over.
The cloisters were black with sleep,
But under the eaves the young were whispering
What has always been whispered
In love's arms.

The men in bowler hats
Lifted you through the door.
They had had a care
For something not quite right
At the edge of vision
And bundled to help.
How they burst the room open
With their red faces and burly shoulders!
How round they were in their constancy!
And you, happy and laughing and cracking jokes
With these men so vivid
They crackled the air.

O gentle men, extraordinary in ordinary,
Squaring the circle, opening the door,
Kind trumpeteers for the entrance of the dying
The boisterers of let's have one more celebration, sir!
Kinsmen of going and wine.

So the task was completed.
The messengers raised their hats
In acknowledgement and closed the door.
For many hours then the throngs of the thanksgivers
Came close about us; all said that was necessary,
Carried to the full cup.
All the compassions of a life gathered
Ready for the juncture,
That supreme night
Burning with the fruit of the honey bee.

In the Mountains of the Monédières, by the Green Waters of the Vienne

In the mountains of the Monédières
I sat by the brook and waited for you.
The young goats came to see
And the pipits dipped all along the watercourses.
On a sudden I thought:
This is how it will be when he never returns.

The silver birch shook her glory over the garden.
Then I saw the book of your thinking
Fresh at the window and heard your voice speaking
The proof of God to me in the early morning
And how we lay talking many hours in his arms.
Your words stepped out of the hills and the foreign houses:
Love is the compact of the art of living,
The art of dying is the art of learning how to love.

* * *

Now I sit by the green waters of the Vienne.
The chalk dust rises as on horsemen long ago.
Waiting for you is past.
It is impossible for me now to rekindle
The desolation of imagining my own desolation.
My love's going was beyond all imaginings.

Suffering changes fears.
The search becomes different,
The road more extraordinary.
In the grapple with time in the clearing
I learnt the wrong questions bring no disclosures.
But she has grown civiller since I assented
To the disciplines of extremity.

Now by the waters she gestures.
Upon the other bank I see
A dark thing, angular, silhouetted,
With obscene attachments hanging
From it like bits of bone.

It is the place where mercy is spent into the sand,
Where our hearts inhabit the delay
Between event and understanding,
The time in which we have to wait
For time's reply.

Discerning at dusk is not easy –
A generality, a ghost –
To fancy a scaffold's become a rooting tree
Is facile assurance.
How can we trust what we cannot see?
Time is a wraith transforming by the waters,
Not what she was, for we can no longer be:
Things change, are wrought in silence,
And come to sit within our soul.
In the shadow where she moves, a white scent grows.

* * *

Evening has come. The green waters of the Vienne
Flow slow as honey; the turtle doves call
As they called long ago. A rhythm
Out of stillness fills the waiting air.
Over the breeze come voices
That are the heart's tug and fall
Of recognition; love's work
The notes that make this music
Into what we shall become.
Only time mothers this chance
To turn what we've received
Into healing.

By the green waters of the Vienne
I hear the hymn of the heart sing to me.
Love is the compact of the art of living,
The art of dying is the art of learning how to love.

Figeac la belle

I remember a marketplace
O Figeac la belle
The bustle and laughter and summer cries
The little, shimmering well.

I remember a marketplace
Where we walked arm in arm,
Where branches danced and the river danced
And lovers were free from harm.

I remember a marketplace
And how we stopped stock still;
Over the breeze came music
From a sudden, haunting hill.

Over the breeze came music.
Five men sat in a row,
Jackets of green and fiddles,
And gold flashed from their bow.

Gold flashed from their teeth and eyes
And black from their sleek hair;
Up and away from them flew their sound
Into the golden air.

They bent their heads together
And their feet tapped the floor;
Their smile passed quick as a javelin
As the sound began to soar.

They struck the air together;
Time and beat were one.
The key and chord leapt asunder
On the finest of patterns spun.

As their sound began to soar it went
Into another land
And all the listeners hung on the thread
Thrown by their flashing hands.

They bent their heads together;
Their feet tapped the floor.
Round and round streamed the melodies
Out of the angel store.

The light grew long round the shadows
As the song sprang to and fro
And the lovers danced to hear the sound
Of the players' brimming bow.

In the marketplace at Figeac
Five fiddlers threw wide the door;
Our hearts flew up into a golden tree
And sit there evermore.

The Old Tram Road

I walked out of the house into spring
And on to the old tram road.
All was by chance when first I came here
Too early for a meeting: a way-sign,
A whim, a turn of the wheel,
The water and the valley unexpectedly before me like a star.
Walkers in the sunshine rested their legs outside an inn.
The barmaid was friendly; I ordered lemonade.
Time grew glassy. Maybe I dozed…

Suddenly there before me my dead friend rose up
Talking, as at that breakfast long ago,
Of life and how to live it.
Mostly we laughed, exchanged stories,
But ravelling down came something stranger
That we both saw together: like recognising
In a distant, unfamiliar structure
A place we knew, but hadn't understood.

'So' – you spread your fingers on the table –
'We can change the past.
I don't mean time running backwards –
The horse jiggled back over the stile,
The spilt milk gone without a murmur back into its jug –
That's philosophical claptrap.

Nor is it just memory, or only its part
In uncovering this, the pattern:
Time is a shuttle weaving back as well as forwards,
Past into future, our future into our past.'

We never sat at a table again, yet now you are here
For a moment to say this. Bees quiver in the lavender.
A little marker points along the old tram road.

*   *   *

So I walked out of the rented house
And on to the pathway. Now it was spring,
My legs and heart ready.
The push and poise of hip and foot
Against the earth was joy.
Everywhere butter primroses,
Harebells, bluebells, fans
Of cow parsley, the daffodils' sun trumpets,
Garlic blooms like snow.
A white house stood above a stream.
Here and there dogs, and their owners' greeting
Gone beneath the trees.

The track turned. Before me stretched a long grove
Of shadow. I waited. At her boundary
The grove also waited.
Time fell still and green.
A curl of air. A loop of light.
The whistle of a plover in the wind.
Then from behind me came a rustle,

A movement passed, taking with it
A pale lapping and flickering,
Glimmerings of lime, slate, willow-grey;
All the leaves lifted, bore
Out to the sunlight at the farther end.

I listen. I listen for memory.
But I have no memories in this place.
How far absence of memories is
From memories of absence.
That is a country full of spirits,
Each tree a terrible comfort.
Inhabiting it is where we most wish,
And wish not, to be.
I listen. Is this what you meant
When you said time moves in many directions?
This pure, clear grove and water are where time
Clothes herself differently; here she can only begin
And sends her new companions, not as ghosts
But messengers, into the past.
And the past startles
Like deer at dusk by a waterhole
Scenting a strange kin.

So memory is presence thrown forward
Into the future, not at all what we think of
As that absence of presence –
He is not here, why this empty room –
That grows like a tumour
Into presence of absence:
That happiness which can never come again.

No, memory is also this: the future where
The mind quickens a present that never was,
A present that will never cease
To be worked on by the soul.

*   *   *

By the old red pump
There is a seat. It's a secret place
Because the furze crowds in.
In the creek below the long-discarded boats
Have burst open like coffins.
How massive the true world's sound is.
An ant moves like thunder.
The water's edge is the sip of presence:
The round hill, the clacking masts
And running sandpipers, all are suddenly bright
And shine upon the past.
Dear God, does time really ring so?
Love, who never here made memory,
Steps my gentle friend into the light.
My love, come close beside me,
Let me tell you what we never dreamt of long ago –
That I would carry you into a future
Not of your carpentry or dancing
Yet which you enter and presence fills the land.

The path to Point is a riot of blackberries.
My soul is walking, feasting.
Time touches time at the quay's tilt:
Spring's tide fills the fruit of autumn
Purple in the hedgerows,

And the seed heads blow, aery
As the curlews' footfall upon the living God.
My love, you are here.
Although not ever again in my arms,
Yet we are wound together like the shell
Of the sea creatures' irrefragable witness.

The sun goes over; ebb catches fire.
The light falls long and differently,
And the road has a new face, angled otherwise:
It is time to turn.
I am here again at the grove:
What was the future now comes towards me out of the past.
Where I stand was beyond reach
To that time before but now is part of it.
Time's harmonic sounds
In our soul's tuning.
The trees stir their arms: time is lifted.
Time is lifted up. The octave rings.

*　　　*　　　*

On the Old Tram Road
The walkers and greetings resume.
The dogs run their trails in and out
Of the undergrowth cheerily,
All outwardly unchanged;
Yet a vast and sharp light sits on the horizon.
My love, you have sat with me here
Many hours making a new world
In this place you never saw.

The stone is warm. The wall daisies flutter.
A robin greets me among the drinkers' feet.
Suddenly out of the east – listen –
Comes a great trumpeting:
Fanfare, arrival, a twist of air,
Companion to companion calling
Alleluia and alleluia,
Drawing across the swoop of the sky
Their presence down into the winged water,
Till sunset sounds over the winged shore.

TIME AT TREMEIRCHION

Nothing's an Impossible Predicate

Nothing's an impossible predicate.
How can we approach it,
It being nothing?
On earth indeed it's not possible.
What can this animal in his burrow
Know of it? We can say what it is not.
But not what it is. Is it the absence of something?
Look at the legions, look at the conquerors
Who have thought so.
Threaten a man with being nothing
And you'll soon see him talk.

Yet how can a man become nothing?
I see you point here and there.
A man is not here in this space.
Yet he was.
Why is he here no longer?
Moreover, he was full of intention:
He thought, he strove, he loved.
That is a great deal to say of a man.
It is certainly not nothing.
So nothing's not absence.
Double negatives are entangling
For now nothing's played us one of its tricks
And become something.

I wish this were mere chop-logic
But you know in your bones it is not.
Indeed, one day you will be just bones.
Does that mean you'll be nothing?
Or have undergone the alchemy of bone?
Are bones presence, or absence?
And what is the meaning of this for what you once were?

When the troop returns to the tusks
And the skull under the baobab tree
Look how they grace them with the gentlest of trunk-touch,
Like tears, like garlands. These creatures
Know nothing doesn't exist; when they leave,
They carry with them the soul of their mother
Over the blue, far hills.

Yet still, she is not as she was.
Again and again we return to it,
This taut like a tightrope between what is and was,
What is and is not.

*   *   *

Some solve it this way: a smile sufficient
For the reckoning of being and time.
Thus: think of the picnics with the clouds going over,
The absolute trust in hands, the excitements,
The shrieking shock as you hit the water,
The delicious exhaustion and riding home.
Well, they are not lost. They are out there.
Nothing's extinguished in that dimension
Where space and time are the same.

All you wanted to keep is there in a metaphysical bottle
Not given up to the ocean; but, rather, set in a floating cupboard
Somewhere in the mesh of what was once possible
And may be again.
So the smile comforts: loss is an illusion.
It has never happened.

With this time travellers' counterfeit
Our heart's pierce is annulled,
Dulled to a symmetry of parallels
Where equivalence masquerades as immortality.

* * *

That is its own illusion.
For then this is what hangs in the mesh
With the green chambers of childhood also –
A village summer, and high summer's activities:
An angel hung on a pole, strung for the dive
Into the pyre flicked open by paraffin and a cigarette lighter
To gasps and laughter.
In the fire, the figures snatches, stretches,
Opens wide its arms and starts to scream.
At first disbelief – was only meant as funfair –
But we are rooted in another marketplace
Where fat spatters the crowd
And from the eternal coals
Comes forth a terrible song:

We are the symmetry of space-time,
Pain everlasting,
Time without God,
And this shall be our forever.

Shall Space Be Time?

Shall space be time?
Time spat-forth trigonometry?
To be stretched, squeezed,
Angularised, numericalled,
Upside, inside, downside, outside,
Round-abouted, dough-nutted,
Stringed, creased?
Algorithm, I bow before you,
Logarithmos, let me pay my dues.
Look how the number-junkie plays out
The finger-jumble of the stars
Even unto the lip over which all that is
Will tumble into the reckoning.

Ah, but there's a cost to the pull of equations,
The price of loss demanded by the dark god:
The man in his cabinet jewelled with minerals
Takes these ciphers for consummation
And never guesses that beyond his perimeter
Stretches world upon transfigured world.

*   *   *

But what about the rest of us?
Those confines aren't adequate in the city streets
Of the real. For we are all purposed.

All, not a single one not, even despairing;
Indeed, despair is the measure of purpose,
Purpose askance, purpose halted, lost,
And its deadly end.
Nothing is so meaningless
As meaninglessness.

Look: in through the fences of fear
The she-wolf leads her children;
Under the arc lights and flyovers,
Along the macadamed thoroughfares of danger,
Past stadiums, motorways, back ends of supermarkets,
Arrowing her trajectory towards the hills.
This she does for care, and love is care.
Try telling her or the fighting fish father,
Blowing fresh oxygen over his babies,
That it's all mere utilitarian hijack.
Cant can exist even in the interstices of algebra.

Then, if we are purposed, time as space
Is meaningless. Space's dimension is geometry:
Ask of geometry which is kinder,
Right-angled or equal-legged?
Time is journey: where we are
Incomprehensible without how we have been,
Relational, not relative.
It sounds simultaneously up and down the moment
Even as by the moment we are made.
Time beckons and bears at once
And in this chord she opens.

* * *

It was summer in the great gardens,
The season of parties, blithe;
Time came to me as two friends talking;
We three drank and joked beneath the willow tree,
Twenty, forty years.
The one I knew when young was silver,
The other laughing with a life of bonhomie.
Friends of my soul, you listened
To the purple of youth, of things done obscurely,
And out of desire and not well;
Upon your care my life has turned.
And what is to be said
Of how you opened the door
For the husband I loved?
There is nothing under the sun a man
Can do for another greater than this.
Such care is stronger than fetters or shrouds
And only time shows this.

That is the harmony:
Not in ease, nor clear conscience, nor melodiousness
– Where is the life that's melodious
Anything but occasionally –
But in the structures of understanding
That cannot exist in any other dimension than time.

Tenby, Night

I did see nothing once.
Or something like.
Except that it is not like anything.
But, at extremity, it shows itself briefly,
Like the eyes of a beast glimpsed
In the undergrowth at night.
There, and not there. A glint that kills.

It was dark, and the moon growing.
She was bright as a lighthouse on the soft sea.
Upwards and upwards
The town wound to the spire at its centre
Where time hung,
A vast and jewelled stillness,
A vast and jewelled stillness.
I stood by the window in wonderment
For the lip of eternity fills us with tears.

Then, like some film across my eyes
I thought at first,
That presence dimmed.
The street lights grew watery, the beacon indistinct,
The ebb shrank back into the dark.
Not shadow, nor the night we normally construe;

But lack, lack of light altogether –
The black in caverns when the torch gives out –
The ground of where I stood had vanished,
And now the moon and stars.

I leant out farther. I heard
That I could hear no sound.
Can the sea cease?
She is our heartbeat, mother.
The ear stopped up by the velvet cloak of no acoustic
Is close, very close, to our own cease to be.
It's not that the straining of our senses meets with nothing,
It's that there are no senses left at all.
The tide goes out, one last drain down; then nothing.

I leant yet farther out, and touched another kind of nothing,
My own body with dimensions gone:
In that annihilation impossible
That I or anything had boundaries,
Or what a boundary was.
This strange dilation took thought with it,
And memory, and all begetting,
No time, direction, edge or circumstance.
Where limit ceases, meaning does also.

* * *

Nothing abhors all these
For they are shape, and shape
Is a break, a rupture, a ripple in the cell,
Something of excess and unaccountable,
Self's stir sparking the prodigal,

The unnecessary, the simple leap into be.
One single tremor is enough to cross this threshold
Into the place where no-thing dies.

It seemed a beat passed. Something glowed.
Water over a limpet, a lap upon the sand,
One curlew cry far down the edge of night.
Softly the mist unclosed and rolled away.

There amidst the stars the town shone,
Upward and upward flowering with light.
Its windows were open like candles
And the sea flashed gold as the shoals turned.
I closed the casement.

Nothing did show itself, an instant,
But the truth's not this.
Being abolishes refusal.
How we choose to live
Creation's now and here
Is the mystery:
Whether as nothing, or in darkness,
Or on the lifting of the tide.

Time at Tremeirchion

I

The house with its lights was above me,
Past me the night road ran.
I crossed. But I had forgotten to ask for a torch
For the way up and down.
Now it was black, so black I could not see
Surface or track. Scuffing the earth
To find where it rose was only more stumble.
From hedgerow to hedgerow I groped
And thought how like a drunk I must look.
Look to whom? What did it matter,
One tiny creature bumbling about in the dark?
Each strike of the thorns was startling and strange.
My steps a bird's, teetering.
As I passed at dusk, a blackbird had scattered,
Chattering; now I should be glad of her company.
What foolishness not to have seen the treachery
This little path would turn in the dark.

Surely between the trees
The house had moved farther off?
Steeper and steeper it seemed to the mind.
Will this never be finished?

I put my hands out, as if to touch a face –
Far, far back, that lean into arms
That tell us we are home.
A bell sounded.
It hung like an owl in the branches,
The very seize of time.

II

Seven windows stand on St Michael's Rock
Windmills turn in the sea
Sheep and shepherd huddle on the hill
Sap drops from the severed tree

Seven windows rise among the swarm of the rooks
The cattle carry the sky
The headland clasps the sea in its arm
The hawk tracks all in her eye

Seven windows flower to Our Lady of Sorrows
Each colour has its own sound
Blue, blue for the robes of the wood
Red for the apple's wound

Seven windows turn the spokes of pity
Wheel of the broken world
Purple the salve for the waste of pain
And the mouths of the fledgling birds

Seven windows hold time's prism
Still in a silent room
A ladybird sleeps in the Holy Word
The dark jar of the tomb

Seven windows carry the rhythm
Of the time of time itself
The tread of the entering angel
Christ's heartbeat felt

Seven windows stand on St Michael's Rock
Windmills turn in the sea
The cut bough's door bursts green crowns
The seraph towers in the tree

III

Ready in the warm house
And this time carrying a torch
For the dark path through the swooping trees,
I heard a voice. Right at my shoulder,
Gentle, and the faintest touch of hand
To get my attention. 'I forgot it would be dark
And I have no light to go back down the hill.'

The wind was our bearer
And we held tight to each other under the whipping stars.
Behind us, the house of meeting;
Beyond us, a bend we could not see.
– What cover in the undergrowth has the blackbird found? –

We walked without speaking.
Only this common road,
One beam, just once,
On this stretch of tarmac
Between greeting and parting.
By the gate, the rain
Came down like candles around us.
Coat and boots put off in the dark hallway,
She leant and kissed my cheek.
No words. We each closed our bedroom door
And re-entered each her silence.
All night the house sighed tender
The surprise of grace so close.

IN THE CARNON VALLEY

At Manorbier

At Manorbier where the surf booms under the castle
Stands the first church where I desired to go,
And its name is Sant Iago.

                I was neither child nor woman
When I stood at that door. My mother and father
Wandered the graveyard, apprehensive,
For they foresaw delusion enters
By the way of credulity, the seers
Who lie and lead and kill.

Of what was read or sung there that morning
Or of what the preacher said, I remember nothing.
No miracle. No choirs of angels.
Only a wisp of incomprehension
Hung in the air. Outside the path was stony
And listless, and my parents glad at my bafflement.

'Look,' said my father, pointing to a figure
In bathing trunks running to catch the tide.
'No wonder the curate so rushed his sermon.'
We laughed. The day was put elsewhere.

But as the years lengthened,
And time began to bury my dead,
Far from those headlands
The words in the surf grew unerring
And I saw Sant Iago in a wild boat
Pull his silver nets from that sea.

At Ruan Lanihorne

Evening comes on.
The pace is never ours.
This place is like those places in the heart
That shift on an old tide
When the fierce leaf falls –
An old sun, sudden, amongst the oak trees,
A boat sunk years past in cold fields
That wakes in the sting of the sea.

These backwaters bellied with life:
The to and fro of loss and building
A castle on the hill that guarded the haven.
At the end of a furrow you can still make out
The faint lines of a quay.

Evening comes on.
But the pace is never ours.
Look! The rain is just starting to fall,
Fine rain, so fine you can't hear it,
Scarcely see it: only by looking aslant
Through the reeds can you make out its increase.
It falls as if it should be the whole mode of the world.

I heard you died, in a far country,
And are buried there.
What am I to do, hearing that horn in the wood?
The weir is gone beneath the waters,
The spate out of the sweet, dark forest
Vanished, the meadows gorged with salt
And running over to my doorstep in rills,
The farthest edge of what was ocean.

The heart holds close these silent places
Like the swan keeping watch
Among the floating grasses
For his mate who long ago was lost.

River People

Some of them – have you noticed? – hardly ever
set foot on land; the chug and wash to them
are sweet as lullabies rocking cradles;
I saw one once step up on to a quay, stagger
two long seconds before smashing amongst seagulls.
These barges are roomy as floating sideboards,
all manner of hide-away drawers, fold-down beds,
interleaving rockets and latchets.
Occasionally you'll see dogs, stiff as figureheads,
at the prow; bras, knickers, shirts
semaphoring to the wind.
But aesthetics aren't neglected:
just count how many gardens of geraniums
and violets swish over the water.
At dusk, you get the best displays of resourcefulness:
everyone here has in his head
whole maps of shallows and rocks and undertow,
even when the galleys are hot
with pepper from salami upriver, different breads,
onions which have been there and back
hung in regattas. At night comes the time of loving
and despair: the water tastes of earth and oil
when you go in it, and there's always one
who walks to the end in the gorge

where currents are strongest, barely time
to hear the velvet ploosh
before the body's gone down to the ocean.
There are special places where they make love:
the young do it under the cliffs mostly, the old in port,
and the middle-aged favour the softer reaches
where the land widens down to the sea.
But nothing, all the washing and talking
and eating and waiting and dying explains
it like this: the ceaseless silver folding
of water on water, our lives like bright shutters of mist
over the stone seas of the hills.

Road Works

What's stopped us
In the cornfields filled with blue?
The engine tickles. Conversation falls.
The children fret and leap about the car.
Farther up, drivers start to open windows.
One woman's picking flowers.

I spy. Well, what then? One swallow doesn't make.
I know the rest. I espy. The horizon's enormous shimmer.
A little hut with scarecrow. Tall trees.
An old man turning into a mysterious gate.
We're all so curiously still.
The heat begins to glaze. Maybe my head's not so clear.
We all need water.

And then the noonday shifts to rustle,
A sifting in the undergrowth.
Whispering in the tall trees. A goat caught in a thicket.
Bees. What are those drums running on a distant hillside,
Gongs, bagpipes? I glimpse a sunburnt hand,
And shot of leopard in the grasses.
The glade slides upward and around the sky.

What was it stopped us?
The cars have melted in the mirage, drivers vanished.
The wind shears across the cornfields, hishing.
Never walk in the groves at noonday.
Never tempt the gods.

In the Carnon Valley

(The Nebra Sky disc)

Time was once gold in this valley –
Men cast out in a slow line,
Slow and careful as the curlews on the mudflats,
Slow panning, slow sift shifting,
Salt in the channels, crystals, star crystals,
Swinging curl in the wind, wind in the forest,
The gulls' ceaseless breaking lament.
Our ankles shift in the silt,
Deep cold in the trickle of the tide.
The swans are riding the hours like moons.
The lugworms tremble at the planet's passing.
They lean towards their bride.
Nightly earth's animals drag her train across the skies;
They acknowledge her with their finest things:
Horn sliver, seed cloud,
The globe of a mother's belly
Tight round the heartbeat within.
The discs turn, the intercessions.

*   *   *

Time was once gold in this valley –
The bushes' fire and lakes of yellow,
This furnace by the shore.

The sky disc tracks our future's circle,
Gold turns to time
In the celestial metal,
The heaven's intersections:
The rarest of gifts for the rarest of gifts.
Scored threads of gold
To delight the growing and the fading moon,
The ball of space and the dancing stars,
In the slow swing, here, of the water,
In our lives' slow filling,
In the tide's draw,
In our slipping down to heaven.

*   *   *

Time was once gold in this valley –
But the wind has gotten up, is brutal amongst the trees;
Beyond the burial grounds
There is a new sound to the sea,
A churn of grey and foam and black against the shore,
Scourings, undertow, sloops of lead water;
The land has grown dull, sullen.
Pit-pens are where we live now, full of our noises;
Our only vision the light we make ourselves,
For the light of our own minds is dazzling.
The moon goes over us like an episodic machine.

Sweet valley, turn away from us then into the dark,
Where the tide is sister to heaven,
Where what we make with our hands
Is what we make with our souls,
Slow panning our covenant with time,

Why we tethered our sky disc to the stars:
Time is our conversation with the gods.

But we grew careless of their intercession
And they do not tolerate neglect.
When they withdrew, they took time with them,
Left us mere space, the golden fruit
A flat and trivial roundel,
The circling of the heavenly things
Quite pointless mirrors of our own despair.

Time was once gold in this valley –
At dawn, silently, the owl goes hunting souls.

That Morning over the City

That morning over the city appeared a small black cloud
That only children and dogs playing in a certain stretch
Of wasteland in the forgotten sector noticed.
By evening the dogs were restless and some howled,
And from this time the mothers started having nightmares,
Doctors related how patients complained of windowless houses,
Moaned so much the nurses could not sleep.

The following day it had shifted slightly, and let fall
A shower of rain, but unusual, sticky,
Like gum dropping from dying trees.
Those who tasted it became indisposed and were transported,
Briefly, to hospital. Councillors agreed investigations
Should be carried out.

On the third day, at noon, there was a blue judder
Through the air and shortly afterwards communications
With outlying areas were disrupted. Many woke to hear
The screams of sirens now throughout the city.
Soon they became accustomed to tramp and rumble,
A knocking on doors and low conversations.
People concerned themselves more and more
With the price of potatoes and not knowing the colour
Of their neighbour's eye. Gradually encounters grew
Fewer and fewer; those who continued to live

In the crumbling tower blocks were glad
Of the extra space. Broadcasts did monitor
Daily the size of the cloud, but it had long ceased
To be of concern. All trees were now encrusted
With crystals and physicians had learnt
The efficacious distillation of medicines
For all manner of hitherto undocumented complaints.
The survivors considered themselves lucky and new babies
Adapted to the lack of light. When finally the fog closed in
Those who had fled to the hills never looked back.

Errand

He was in the brake, panting.
Needing to get there and bring back news
He saw this too: the scrub oaks
Leering and the mist like oil on his head,
The glimpse of a hart with glowing coals for eyes
Who stood still, watching him.

Remember your errand, news of the kinsman,
Is he alive or dead? Boy, you go, being
Young, outside suspicion. But no regard
For fear which strikes the dumbest,
The most innocent, in the heart of the forest.
The image of it is these eyes, these coals.

We all know fear's curdling noises aren't just chance.
He's plain glad when he smells the farmyard's dungheaps,
Reality of domestic cow led gently to the threshold,
The trail of white spilt casually by the door.
Slowly they turn their brown gaze to him, standing still.

Inside, the chalice pails are carried forward
Through the rows of heroes lying on the floor:
Milk steams in the morning light against their lips;
From their wounds rises red sweat, stains the walls.
Bits of bone, hair, underfoot make the cowherds stagger.

'Found the stricken men there, exhausted, in great number
Gored, and saw the milk carried hot from the kine
For the restoring of their blood;' saw compassion
And its brute occasion in the red white liquids mixed,
The cows with blazing eyes, the hart transfixed with pity.

At Pill Creek

Under the secret, under the dark tree
Past a scrabble of leaves and brambles
And an old hoe stacked against a shed
The path sheers steep down.
Children clamber and chatter
As they carry their toys to the sea,
Enquiring like stars of the stranger
'Did you see our boat at the moorings –
The dark blue and white one, gold stripe –
We're going to paint her.'
                    Twelve rowers pass.
The sea is far out, on the turn.

The eddy turns under the fingers of saltweed
And the black rocks turn, tilted
All one way by a giant's hand –
They're resting for now, but they'll be off soon.
Watch the ooze underfoot: walking the line needs care.
Our edge leads along the overhang of branches;
They dip, pick the tide, string catches
Of bladderwrack up into the breeze
Like shrouds.

Behind us – what was that? – a click,
A plop, odd, like a spick every so often
Into the mud, insistent, particular.

AT PILL CREEK

The water is turning.
Here, look, in their thousands,
Brilliant green acorns, dropped from the cup,
Ready for rooting. Into the rockpools they roll
And amongst the pebbles; and the wide salt arms
Of the sea take them.

A man drives down the causeway
On the opposite bank, unloads tools
Carefully and crosses the plank
That serves as a bridge till the sea returns.
She is fingering the land now,
And the boathouses are alert on their stilts.

Long spools of rope suddenly snake
From the mud as the keels lift.
On his little boat the fisherman
Is looping nets over and over,
Loving his craft amongst the tabernacles
And landing stages; soon we will hear
His outboard motor, see its puff of rancid blue.
Wood doves cluster a last moment
At the sweet source that gushed from the gully:
Remember this, remember where it ran.

A van draws up at the quayside, hastily:
'Pa! Pa! Take me with you!'
The chubby boy runs awkwardly
Across the mudbank, is lifted in,
Hugged and joyful for the rounding
Of the headland in the distance,
Its boundary of blue.

'You can help – watch while I steady her.'
A start. The boat moves out upon the water.
On the seastairs, the stranger smiles and waves.
'Wave! Wave! Do you see him?'
The child laughs, halloos, from the top of his happiness,
Tiptoeing taller and taller to see the figure
Receding to the end of vision,
Arm raised over and over
Each to each under a vast heaven
Till the boat at last rounds the promontory
And the deep comes in.

The Yew at Llangernyw

This yew's so old its centre's turned to air,
Light where the heart strength sprang,
Its trunk pierced open to the other side.
Gentle it sits as a lily flower upon the land
And from its branches children drop and hide.

A little frond curl once, settling
At a chance where rivers rose,
At a shadow between here and after,
The edge cast by what grows
When accident turns to witness.

Snows and fruiting came;
The lattice ever greener and redder
And green and red the worshippers,
Host upon host till the earth grew rich with them
And their seasons' refrain.

The tree carries them now in its crown
– And did you think I would forsake you? —
Spirit and sap are twined to a song
That only in this harmony is
And its birds can never be counted.

In the Neuadd Valley, Bannau Brycheiniog

Here in the hall I first heard it, these mountains a bowl
Of green and golden, blustery clouds
Pouring over the moor. And I lay down
Not far from the horses, and called to them.
Slowly they approached, trusting and not trusting the sound,
Hooves wavering. High above us mewed a bird of prey.
The grasses rustled. It seemed the horses drowsed,
Dreamed. Now a great stillness settled.
And, as we dreamed, red dunes rose up,
Set fast to rock, were eked away by rain and rivers;
Glaciers built, and gouged steep gorges
Down the mountain's flank, then faded
In a rising summer mist.

And yet the horses did not move at all.

At last one mare stepped out, thrust her muzzle close
Till I could feel her hot breath on my hair.
So it began.

Not voice, nor animal cry nor instrument
But something living, making out of time
A sound, as if beyond the thresholds
I could hear the song of all that is,

And me, and horse, and mountain
Were held and threaded on that perfect bow.

What sweetness, sudden and immediate,
Lying in the grass was; just to be
And listen, my mind opening and closing upon eternity.

COMPASS LIGHT

North: York

I travelled north,
A way I didn't know –
Along seams of concrete, girders,
Scraps of paper bowling
Across the high-rise motorways.
Cities rose up – fast motion –
Speed swishing in and out of cars,
Signs, flashes, signs, horizons, concentrate
Or it's death.
                    The land hovers
Just below my sightline, sweeping in and away
On wheels. Placards change dialects
As the armies march. Somewhere,
At a crossroads, on what you might think
Was a nondescript incline, a highway
Loops up across fields from the south,
And, snick, clicks into place just at the apex
Of all that you can see of territory
Over wide England.

                    Then I reached the bridge.
From far off its back rises, smooth as a nerve.
My road tracks towards it like a lashing tail,
No unloosing now the curve, tied, taut
To the swerve of the water. With a jolt
My car shoots over the join and is launched,

Up, up, soaring, nothing up here but air
And struts like strobes streaking the sea
Into lightning. What ramparts
Shift across the heavens, visions.

*   *   *

I have arrived in the northern city.
Car parks, roundabouts. Gates. Security.
My lodgings are cement and steel.
Here is a lake, and ducklings,
Geometric trees around the edge.
I notice the walkways return like mazes.
Now obligation bustles me
To the task I must attend.
Traffic into the centre,
A square, where criers gather
To tell their stories; in the glare a glint
As of swords, and men shouting acclamation,
The clatter of hooves setting off
Across continents to carry the news.
Such things happened here.
Our little church squats like an afterstone
Upon that tide.

We take our seats
And bustle with our programmes.
Four men in black enter, their faces sober.
I had expected instruments, not knowing.
That little silence before time begins.

*   *   *

Language's frontier
What is the language here
Four voices together
Into one chord

Four voices together
The ringstone, the harmony
Harmony is the rood tree
On which hangs the soul

Harmony is the rood tree
Our high bird in the canopy
Like rainfall on sunlight
Lets fall his song

Like arms in the sunlight
The branches lift rainbows
Raise here and no elsewhere
The apse of the soul

Raise now and no elsewhere
The arch of abundance
Up and down to heaven
In the heartwood

Up and down to heaven
From the dark root's base
Where the skull and the human heart
Make a chord of grace

West: Wells

I travelled west.
Over the lanes and chalk downs of England
– Blossom lies heavy along the banks of the Frome –
It was the time of Our Lady,
The latest of our conversations.
She is as patient as the springs that drop
Down through the rock
Before they come to light.
While we lay sleeping
The rain trickled,
The waters moved in the clefts.
All the spans needed
For what I saw ripple up between reeds
And green lilies, a pool of growing water,
Globes, loops, haloes rising,
Out of her heart flow fountains,
Out of her wells life.

* * *

For you this house was built
Before ever you were born
Mightier than any bone
But bone-bred, bone-thought
Thought which uncovers
Boundlessness in stone

A soul-built spine
Though its wagon here was bone
Souls hang upon this scaffolding
Flesh raises dreams
Lines on a draughtsman's board
Stitch heaven's seams

Out of the earth grow arches
The labourers sweat prayer
Their arms carry the building's cross
Cut in infinity's air
Yet who can tell where underground
Those arcs meet?
Time hides the close of that ellipse
But the soul lies there
A bow is not a bow
Without the force that draws it
The arrow goes through the one opening
Time toward time bestows

South: Notre Dame de Livron

We travelled south –
To the high guard's tower:
From the rooftop
The territory blazed.
It ticked and sighed at noon.
O the high bird's mew in the forests!
Down into the shelving combes
The land bent away like a bow.
Out of the dust into the damp dell
The pathways grow.

Sing and walk.
By Bonnette's stream the trees leave
Indigo over the rock.
Amongst the mosses
Two damselflies, their dance:
Curled abdomens in ecstasy
Union's trance.
Through dark fern and woodrush
The ewes clack down
The angels' trackway to drink.

Little Bonnette bounces
From bluff to bluff to bluff
And green hurtles in her wake.

Chapels lean over to see,
The mill wheels rejoice.
We were in our summer
The soul's summer, feet on the road,
Breezes – why do they make us wild so
With their longing? And stir from a place
Impossible to reach but true?
Bonnette chirrups in her valley
Answering the inquisitive birds.
Gaillarde, will you tell me your story?
The rondel of water
Repairs the earth's cry,
Our rooted ache. Sister water,
We cluster to you like children –
In your arms cradle us,
Sing us that song of assuage.

By the fountain
Bonnette sits in her robe of blue
Under the smooth platania trees.
Air lights the insects' halo.
We have built our love for her
On this little plot.
A bell hangs in the branches.
Bell of the time when the mountain ranges
Were carried away in the beak of a bird.

We let our hands into the water.
Folly and joy are met together
In the spring's tongue,
In the sunlit channels.

The women talk in the shade
And the children run.
The fruit is here in the still instant
Overhanging the water.
Do not reject our prayer
Nor withhold your love from us.
The chapels settle a little
In the falling sun.
Bonnette greets us, and passes;
Arm raised, and gone.
Her beam rises upon her territory.
In the valley below she turns her course
Drift upon drift through shade and sunlight
Dancing to the dazzled cliffs and infinite
Down to where glory darkens
Under deep Noble Val.

East: Canterbury

We travelled east –
Your youth's citadel.
The arrow of the road
Points the end of summer.
Atop the warm steps
The casual boys sling arms
Across shoulders for the photograph.
Their gaze arrives at the little gaggle
We make upon the grass.

You are dying:
At the held hand
Your daughter's cheeks flush.
This is how you will remember her.
At the cornerstone
Spirit takes the strain:
The whole building rises upon it.
Once there was nothing here but meadow.
Now in the shadow
We hear you breathing,
Slow, marked.
Your daughter is attuned
As she never will be again
To the in-and-out draw
Of how we leave life;
The wail of the broken embrace.

This man in his agony sings
Who jousted with his fellows,
The fair-haired gods gone under the ground.
O salus mea! At the edge of life
Where the singers pass
Its colours sound back to us;
The lyrebirds of wisdom
Spread their wings
To hear the note.

Tell, my tongue,
Of the sad glory of living,
Of the burning evenings
And the dew on the hawthorn,
The glance of a lover,
The scent of gardens at night.

Young men and maidens
Lean heads together,
Meagre place where the sacred begins.
How they stare to hear
The song of the exercise of death,
The ravening discipleship,
Its desert sorrows.
When men purpose a trench
To raise their edifice in the wild fields
Silence listens;
Under the stone floating
An angel's fingertip.

Friends have gathered;
Your daughter's eyes glitter in your presence
Like a gemmed casket.
Love begets faith
And faith begets perception.
We believe in the face of all the evidence
And then find that the evidence has changed.
This is not easy metaphysic,
Nothing to do with the philosophers of surface
For whom the curtain of the instrument
Is all there is of real.
Love's attentiveness quickens:
Remember the little boy with no brain
Whose soul grew back miraculously?
Love did this.
Imperception bears no children,
Is its own wall;
Inert does as inert sees –
Never detects the tremor in the stone.

The singers have arrived at the reach of darkness.
They struggle with the difficult words.
The lyrebirds stir and glance.
Tell, my tongue,
Of when the human senses fail.
At the utmost rim
Love's longing rises
Upon the field of God:
The mind intent,
This sudden place shimmering
And rushed with colour,

Seed, flower and berry
At one instant on the tree.
Love's life fills full
In end and opening:
The vessel dances
In her disciplines
Before the gates of God.

OCTAVE FOR OUR LADY OF TIME

I
Advent

All life is advent.
Why did a man in a cell write this?
It wasn't, though it would be easy to think so,
The certainty that he was to be taken out
And hung. For, as a boat travels upon death,
He had been sailing this element his whole life.
When the swell rises, the mariner acts, not thinks,
What to do: the hand, the keel, the wind
Sing together, because they have sung together
Many times before, and knowing they will part
Is not part of it.

All life is advent.
Nothing to do with fate:
That's a lazy thing, a fairground pastiche,
A screen where artificial gods pop up
And burst, for no reason.
Doubtless you've spotted the paradox:
Chance *is* in there, the swing that could go
Right or left as the evening takes us
But the anonymous traveller
Who sat five minutes beside us
Between King's Cross and Angel
Won't ever return.

So, is it spontaneity?
Of a kind. A dancer rehearsing
Her steps, winter, summer, winter, alone,
With long rain at the window,
Readying herself for the incomparable alliance,
The meeting of moment and the heart's perception
When honeysuckle opens the night.
Her secret is, the miracle may come, or never.

All life is advent.

II
Ingatestone

I parked among the meadows.
It was the summer of prohibition, fear.
A bench stared, empty –
Touch carries the plague –
In the distance, anxious lorries thundered
The old road. But the trees waved blithely:
Remember splendour.
A couple made off surreptitiously
Across the fields to hide
In the forgiving grass.

O lady on the wall, you beckon:
Your stiff gaze is tender in the stone.
We are debtors but care not a fig
As we lie in the gardens
For your generosity into the future,
Plans for the mind laid out on your table
At evening, repose of the spirit
In a bedside flame.

Maybe callousness is in fact the first sin –
Lack of gratitude,
Lack of gratitude for everything.

Life discloses
The truth of the clocktower:
Sans Dieu Rien.

Just my feet on the gravel
Under its shadow
And my soul listening.
The scatterings are very fine:
Flint flecks – fork clatter on a plate,
Goods loading, a wave, a kiss,
A daughter departing.
The way she turned her head.
Slivers that lie here form lives;
Foundations rustle,
The revolutions hum.

How much forgiving is needed
That we know nothing of, words
Said in desire, spite, casual wounds,
Old quarrels, contexts, preoccupations.
Do the heartstrings start still
At the crack of a stair?
Will we always stumble in the ha-ha
Between touch and touch?

Silence is never no sound.
Not even in death.
Silence waits upon the question
We cannot articulate:
A man, a woman kneel here,
Refining the approach again and again

Like the embroiderer
Whose pattern comes in the doing of it,
Whose antiphon includes the silence,
Whose silence is the weave,
The respond:

The look away, the shut ear
The truths kept mum, the facts invented

The emotions sunk in stealth, the dispossessions
The lapse from honour, the insufficiencies

The grand illusion
Our own stealing from the room

* * *

A company enters the upper gallery
– Light falls on summer lawns –
Linenfold holds the secret.
Tenacious petitioning that begins
When these friends take their places.
One man sounds the note beneath his breath,
Bright sorrow like a bird in his memory,
His wife holding grief in a cup,
Their fellows each with the book of entreaty
Open in front of them.
We have abandoned ourselves often enough
By our lack of care;
We have pulled the curtains of complacency,
Sat in our avarice.
We built as others fled into the night.

Done can't be undone: that is the child
Saying wish, wish, wish.
How could there be any mending
Unless a readiness to admit it?
Adulthood is getting down on our knees.
Counterpoint this new song with mercy:
We pray for light to come again upon the lawns.
Under the steadfast clocktower
We sing our unceasing canon:
Forgive, forgive, forgive, forgive.

III
King Harry Ferry, Trelissick Passage

A ribbon of road is glory:
The lightning of the foliage in spring.
Stars flash from the granite:
I saw them last night in the wave of heaven.
Now they are everywhere,
Yellow, and blue, and white.
They are poured out over the banks,
They crowd like speartips.
How many shades of green can you see in the wood?
Lime for the first shoots that float,
Lemon for the sharp touch in the undergrowth,
Olive for the shadows that hold us.

Fiery green woods!
Your arms are full of life.
The children are in the glades again;
The hollows echo with their somersaults,
By the hidden waters,
By the crossing point.
The doves send out their love-calls
Over the treetops like incense.
Now, at the little spit of land,

The ferry clanks towards us.
Its blue bulkhead is crazy with promise:
Seagulls and dreams and the signalling crabs
Bristle with it. The bunting on the deck
Streams away into the forest;
It winds a glory around the sun.

The cars back up, press against the barrier
With their desire to get to the other side.
It's hot, even in the breeze that's come from nowhere;
The horizon shimmers.
Time enough for lovers to rest upon the parapet
Their rose hopes, to fly out from the clumsy ark
Into the haze and bring back
One bright sprig of spring.

IV
At the Sea Wall

Dawn unwraps the town –
Dun-grey, slate-grey, pale oyster-light;
In the air, like a veil, fine rain.
Mussels and whelks tick
As the tide turns around;
They must weather out the tender time
When the wrack hangs on the harbour stair,
When the nets are picked over.
It's vertiginous down to the bilge and plastic bottles
Scumming the sluices; clam-cold
The planks are stacked like bones.
A saw screeches in the repair sheds,
Paint and turpentine and salt sweat
Everywhere here under the fog's tarpaulin.
You can hardly see beyond your hand,
Not even the promontory light
Nor the lifeboat station.
Out of sight, the sea rocks like a whale sleeping.

*   *   *

Gently the traveller comes along the quay,
Stepping with care amongst the ropes and chains.

Will the boats run
In the great fog?

The horn is sounding far out across the bay
And the hour, too, from the island,
Calling and warning, sisters.
The tongue in the harbour chapel trembles
Remembering the journeys –
Foodstuffs, clothing, remedies,
Never knowing rightly for how many –
As they came and came
Down the hill on to the grey shore
And got the tough blessing of the ferryman
Shouting and trying to sort them.

Will the boats run
In the great fog?

In the bleak oyster-light,
On the desert sea?

The lifeboat has slithered down the slipway
And is circling on invisible patrol.

*   *   *

The sea, the sea
Each man dreamt it
On the wherries
Long ago

The wash against the keel
At dead of night
Stars' swell
And compass light

Ocean's rising ever falls
Down the purple deep
In the skeltering gale
Terror and truth meet

Sailors' entreaty
The rigging's cry
No unbelievers
On the sea's vast eye.

* * *

Gently the traveller comes along the quay:
Andrew and Peter Morgan,
Boatbuilders by the harbour wall,
Have a fine smack almost ready.
They're smoking and cracking jokes;
Maybe their wives will come down later.
But this newcomer wants passage –
He has been asked to go to the island –
They can all hear the bell.
He sits on the wall, scraping shapes in the dust
While they discuss him.
Lack of wind's not the problem
With an engine, and radar,
In theory, lifts the fog's veil.
Yet why, in this weather?

Why risk the channels
As they suddenly change,
And everyone knows
The unexpected always arrives?
Beyond the jetty
Fishermen clatter their lobsterpots.
A lathe turns, somewhere.

Then silence. Even the seagulls are silent.
A breath, a look, a cigarette butt in the water.
The moment's abundance.
Carefully, the traveller descends the sea ladder
And they wrap him in their coats.
The normal bustle, untyings and stashings of things
Ready for the harbourmaster's light.
It is time. The bell sounds continuously
Out of the cloud. It is time.

* * *

Round the sea wall, the boat dips into her channels,
Grey upon the swell, and tilting slightly
As the world shifts to the weight of her cargo,
That faint breath from her prow,
A whisper lighting the sailors' hair.
In readiness, the island gathers up her multitudes,
The sheep in the heather lift their heads,
The children in the schoolyard hesitate,
The wracked trees lean towards the water:
Is it true?

AT THE SEA WALL

Out of the stillness the sound of voices
Glances as a note off glass,
Ringing beneath the surface.
A finger ripples along the shore
And the sea's grain flickers
Like mackerel rising
To array the boat
With all her shining outriders
Inquisitive for the upper air.

V

At the Underground Gate

The hole lies open.
It never shuts.
The steps down are polished
By the tread of feet,
The unending passing.
In this place there is nothing
That does not have as its purpose
The facilitation of transience:
The sleek rectilinears,
Icons, blips, ricocheting ticket barriers
Through which all tilt and go.

Zizz on the moving walls too –
Home insurance health endurance,
Webuyanycar Justeat
Lose ten pounds in three weeks
Your dream holiday cure your baldness
Wear a mask find love
Gamble responsibly SANITISE!

The escalator's silver-black dizzies –
In the depths a shuttle is coming
A shuttle is coming a shuttle is coming

To whisk off your head
Sway forwards jolt back lurch right pitch left,
Sway back jolt left lurch forwards pitch right;
Every face is bent over the non-stop mesmeric
Held in the palm of a hand.
Surrender is already forgotten—
When you've adjusted for loss in advance,
No loss remains to adjust to.

Going somewhere else? We all are.
Our souls rattle away
Down the tunnels of perpetually evacuated time.

* * *

I saw him here, at the underground gate.
Day after day, a bird perched on a rock
In a flood, a dipper dipping into the indifferent stream.
Dip, dip; dip, touch, dip; dip, dip.
'Good morning ma dame'. The words held out like pebbles
Scrubbed clean of scurf, shining, ma dame,
My lady, day after day, a precious thing he had made.

One day I halted, stepped out of the flow
And bought what he offered,
For your bright eyes, my lady:
Speak to me out of the stream of strangers
In your tongue that's not mine
But we share. Where do you come from?
Where are you going? He held out the change
To me, and I saw his bundle tucked under a withered arm.
The flood poured past us and vanished.

So it began. I looked for him
Each time the bus snapped open
And I stepped out.
He was a very precise courtier.
I mean *this*: he stood at the gate
And greeted all those who passed,
Whether they turned to him quick eyes or dead.
Our exchanges grew:
The tiny rags and rustles of friendship
By the descending stair.

One day, his face full of light,
He held up his picture excitedly for me,
His image, his story printed:
'My name is Abdar.
I come from Albania.
At birth my mother rejected me
Because of my withered arm.
A cousin raised me.
No apprenticeships:
For what good is a man with only one arm?
But I can be an assistant,
Help in the shop, reach for things,
Remember the customers and what they like,
See their worries,
Hear their tragedies.
No chance with young women
But a widow took me. She had three children.
I helped bring them up. Then she left us.
Her children are mine now.
How to get enough money?

A friend wrote, "Come to England.
I have work for you. Well paid."
So I came. But he was not here.
I work selling this. I am homeless
But they have been good to me.
Soon I may have my own flat.
I send my money back to my children.'

Courteous Abdar, teach me what you knew,
Who astonished me, being so true.

*   *   *

Then plagues came. Speckled winds
Swept over the cities;
Hatred danced upon the platforms.
Sickness crept after through the marketplaces,
In shadow, door to door.
The streets emptied. Love's touch turned to fear.

On a winter's afternoon I walked alone:
The canal half frozen, the barge sails
Stuck stiff and red against a white sky.
It seemed my feet were the only thing that moved.
And yet as I moved the sails moved with me
Their angles altered
And all around them altered;
The landscapes hark us back, but never take us back.

A mile on, I came to the underground gate
Chained shut. The void boulevard stretched away.
Suddenly I felt a dip in the air,
'Ma dame' in the frosty trees.

Ah yes, he will have been whirled away,
Like so many others, as they were in those times,
And lost, or returned to his country.
And maybe survived, or died, and is buried
Where a shepherd carries his lamb
On a dry hillside.

VI
O Magnum Mysterium

Time, that is, grace and circumstance
Acting on our good will.
Circumstance handed me this sentence.
I took it and went to sit
In the lee of a hill
With my back to a tree.
There was a scent of wet and wild garlic
But the wood behind me
Was still of wind and birds.
Deep to deepening still.

How do we reach into silence?
You cannot touch it, nor hold it, nor pour it.
You cannot describe it
For words snuff out silence.
That's when it most eludes.
But to believe by that
It is nothing
Is to mistake ungraspability
For absence.
Water, being formless
And tasteless and colourless,
For all that moves mountains.

Makers of music know this:
Chords spring out of the span of silence
Not from empty space
Across which a rat may scuttle.
The drummer in equipoise, waiting,
His arms upturned to the air;
The conductor also,
Holding all expectations
On the tip of a wand.
In silence forces reveal themselves
Like creatures who fly only at dusk,
Far more intimate to us
Than we can ever be.

This was the circumstance.
Here at the rough bole of the tree
Upright on the hillside:
Deeper and deeper into its branches
The onrush of the sky,
Heaven's blue dowry.

The leaves listened.
Not a sigh.

Then the tree opened
And I saw through the bark
Living fire in channels
Going up and down;
The tree was a flowing column:
Green, amber, gold
Plunging and rising;

Salamanders and dragonflies
Played at its core.
Out of its branches deltas of light
Spread over the green ground.
And yet the trunk stood taut and still
Even as its body teemed.
Earth's hearth and air's fall
Bounded in the grace of time
In the tree.

So it may be when a woman sits
In a room alone
Her thoughts open by the lily-blown window
And, on a sudden, feels
The downdraught of heaven within her.

VII
The Pole of the World

Marie-Ange looks at her watch.
Everything ready:
Cleaned, checked, put back correctly.
That's the discipline.
We do this together, a team,
Like assembling an aircraft
Or raising a house.

How many oxygen canisters?
Fire extinguishers?
Can the cranes extend to their full height?
Ladders. Thermal cameras.
And the medical equipment. In place.
All communications systems working,
And ourselves – are we polished, prepared
For the inspection; for the siren; for the first time?
We never know when the hour.

*   *   *

Easter, the year's apex.
The buildings have their arms wide open to the sky.
Under its bridges flows the Seine.
Holidays are in the air: ministers are closing

Their offices and palaces. Tourists take photos.
A prelate is taking his coffee
Outside a café and enjoying the breeze.
His friend the proprietor lingers at his table.
It's the ease at the day's end
And the shadow's fall.

Everything's still in the rafters, the stillness that settles
Straight away after the sounds of the workmen
Fade on the stair, an idling, the fag-ends of endeavour –
Dust from the mighty transoms,
A scrap of sandpaper, carpenter's wood-curl, maybe,
Floating towards the spark.
Far below at the back of the precinct
The security man's doing his rounds
In the dark; isn't sure where
Or whether he heard a bell.

Across the street, a functionary closes her computer
And starts packing her desk for the break.
As she bends for her briefcase
Something catches at the edge of her eye, unfamiliar,
Is there that was not there before –
A streak of grey, a feather,
Movement where no movement should be.
At its base, like a kitten's tongue,
The tiniest dab of orange.
Now she's at the window:
Simultaneously, she notices, along the quayside,
The lovers and cyclists and joggers are all standing still.

*　　*　　*

'Eight minutes into the stair.
Eight minutes since we stood in our courtyard,
Machines gleaming. Into the stair
No wider than a man,
And where the only thing in sight
Is your colleague's boots, so close you can touch them,
Disappearing above you up into the darkness,
Into the tightening spring of the spiral.
Our shoulders bang against the wall –
It's hard to climb with sixty pounds of armour on your back.
It's hard to breathe. This stair was only ever
Meant to lead to a mason's prayer;
His sinews twist around us,
The walls glow. We're at the door.'

*　　*　　*

'Behind it, the forests that came in ox-carts
From Compiègne, from Ermenonville,
The glades of birdsong to give us our roof
On whose beams men nested.
Weeks to shape the curves
Where the nightjars had churred
Into our lady's bower.
The leather bags came from the tanners
And it was time.
Jerked heavenwards – yes, we all joked –
Like parcels of flesh to be weighed
But some of us always shat ourselves out of fear.
Dear God! What you see when you're up there:
The cities of the world in a blue shimmer,

The angels talking. Their gantries
Criss-cross our dreams.
Around you whips the wind,
Howls and tugs you into the flying air.
Yet on a gentle day I swear it brings
Meadowsweet and apples.
Slowly we closed the housing.
By the end of it none of us recognised
The new carpenters, nor how they did things:
But they hang from Our Lady's rooftop
Just the same.

At night, when we're gone,
She especially sits here
Within the forest we made for her
At the top of the winding stair.
She sits, and listens,
And the city's cry rises to her.'

* * *

How seeming frail is the rod to heaven:
Stones crack and ring; the gargoyles budge
Amongst the cherubim.
The spire's burnt through:
Her cloak of sparks lifts into the air.
What wind of flame is in the angels' wings.
O sombre meeting.
We run like ants along the walkways:
'Get back! Get back!'
Her spine trembles a moment against the dark,
Bows, snaps, brings down like thunder
The tonnage of the sky.

Into the gloom.
The uprush of breath has slammed the doors.
From the crossing's eye
Lead pours in streams
And on the blue buds of paradise
Strange salts settle.
Hanging from the vaults
The men of words have become invisible:
Soot is in our mouths; our crowns burn.
Water and fire are at the city gates,
The engines turn our foundations to putty.
When the keystone fell,
The towers lifted up and out of true.
Upon their battlements
The night creatures lean out
And chatter, curious; a smoke plume
Strakes across the rooves.
An easterly's got up
And drives towards the bells.

*   *   *

Emmanuel
Great bell
Sounding hark
And knell

Bourdon
World drum
Hung from the tree
Heaven swung

Bourdon
Earth thrum
Soul's song
Stars' tongue

Emmanuel
Dark bell
Sounding save
And farewell

* * *

It's two in the morning.
The night is cool. Along the street
Marie-Ange and her companions jostle each other
Good-naturedly in and out of the gutter,
Drink in great gulps from their water bottles.
They hail others who recognise them
And who turn to look back as they pass.
Their helmets are burnt black,
Their arms heavy from hanging all night in the fire.
Behind the windows of blues and gardens
They saw rise up those angels dancing.
Now the breeze from the river comes over them,
Like water running in fountains, running over the rim.
The captain touches his young recruit's shoulder;
This night none of them will be eager for home,
For sleep, instead of this hour in the furnace.
This night their barracks are their exaltation.
They shower, and clean their uniforms,
Take leathers to every filthy buckle,
Restore each fragment lost inside the tower.

Grease, smoke and stone dust have caked the fire engine:
To make her spotless will take the whole night's watch
Till roll call at morning.

Far off, the sirens drift into the dark.

Marie-Ange sits in silence on the bench;
The faces of her friends are lit up, beyond exhaustion:
Men raised aloft, orderlies hustling away the holy things,
Those who held the door against doom,
Those who grasped the rungs of pity.
Eyes shut, she steps again into the coil of the stair
– The first time, her first time,
Like a child on the brink of the mystery,
Seeing the stars and the prophets circling,
The pole of the world stained with fire.

VIII
Walking the Analemma of the Soul

As when you look at the sky
And the constellations you knew are all at once
The same and entirely strange.

I walked the rim of a great bay at evening.
The wave lifted just a hush upon the shore.
Before me lay the sea's blue discus;
Above me the salt birds died away.
As night came in, only this edge
Between the worlds remained
Opening upon footstep,
Disclosing like dusk flowers.

Then began the brilliance, slowly.
Hour and immortal rose together:
The cup of moon, the sparks, the milky traverse,
The immense play of heaven moving forward
Out of the dark.

In rapture, the land leant forward
And, in the breach between two paces,
Took sea and sky tenderly into her arms.

And those two great arcs of all we know
Gazed upon each other
As on a beloved's face.

Embrace and reply turn time's helix,
The upstroke and cross-stroke
Where one note is always also two and three,
Is never alone.
Listening for this is the work of living:
How we walk with our dead
While they are living;
How we will walk with our living
When we are dead.
For dust is never finished with conversion,
The Holy Ghost music
That is the unfolding of love and time.

All we can carry away from this earthly life
Is that which we have given away –
So may we come into the great praying,
So may we come into the great prayer.

As when you look at the sky
And the constellations you knew are all at once
The same and entirely strange.

Notes

'Chasms': the modern Greek spelling of Arcadia is 'Arcadía'. The 'd' is pronounced like the 'th' in 'though' and the accent falls on the last 'í', thus : 'ArkathEEa'. This is different from the pronunciation more commonly used by non-Greeks, 'ArCAYdia'.

'The Dead of Chorion: 'Leonidas' pronounced 'LeonEEthas'; 'Taygetos' : pronounced 'TaIgetos'.

'The House on the Hill': 'evcharisto' is modern Greek for 'thank you'.

'At Manorbier': the name for St James in Welsh is Sant Iago, as in the Spanish.

'In the Carnon Valley': the Nebra sky disc is the world's oldest known portable depiction of the heavens. It was found in 1999 by metal detectorists near Leipzig. The gold used to represent the sun, moon and stars has been shown by geochemical analysis to originate from the Carnon Valley, Cornwall, where it was probably extracted by panning.

'Errand': the quotation is from Sir John Wynn, *History of the Gwydir Family and Memoirs* (Gomer Press, 1990).

'The Yew at Llangernyw': this yew tree is believed by dendrochronologists to be between 4,000 and 5,000 years old, making it one of the oldest living organisms on earth.

'Compass: North': 'the apex/Of all that you can see of territory/ Over wide England': this is High Cross, where the Roman roads of Fosse Way and Watling Street meet. It lies about seven miles south-east of the site of the battle of Bosworth Field, and is very near the geographical centre of England.

'Compass: South': the Bonnette is a small tributary of the Aveyron, which it meets at the town of St Antonin Noble Val. The Livron is itself a tributary of the Bonnette.

'Ingatestone': the site of a Tudor manor house belonging to the Petre family. The daughter of its first owner and builder, Sir William Petre, founded Wadham College, Oxford, under her married name of Dorothy Wadham. Her half-brother was the patron of William Byrd, who wrote many of his late mass settings for the family.

'At the Underground Gate': some of the details in this poem were inspired by a story in *The Big Issue*, 6–12th May 2019.

'The Pole of the World': several of the factual details in this poem are drawn from Brigade de Sapeurs-Pompiers de Paris and Romain Guibert, *La Nuit de Notre-Dame par ceux qui l'ont sauvée* (Grasset, 2019) and Claude Gauvard, *Notre Dame de Paris, The Eternal Cathedral* (Editions E/P/A, 2019). Emmanuel is the name of Notre Dame's largest bell.

'Walking the Analemma of the Soul': an analemma is an asymmetrical figure of eight that represents the migration of the sun's position in the sky seen from a fixed location at the same solar time but on different dates over a year.

I am indebted to Victor Zuckerkandl's work, *Sound and Symbol, Music and the External World,* Princeton University Press, 1973, for his insights into 'the miracle of the octave'.

Acknowledgments

Grateful acknowledgments are made to the Royal Literary Fund, a Fellowship from whom allowed part of this collection to be written. Some of these poems formed a portfolio that was shortlisted for the Michael Marks Environmental Poet of the Year Award 2023; 'That Morning Over the City' was commended in the Winchester Poetry Festival Competition 2024. Thanks also to the editors of the following journals where some of these poems first appeared: *Agenda*, *PN Review*, *Poetry Salzburg*, *Scintilla*, *Temenos Academy Review*, *The Oxford Magazine*, *The Tablet* and *Wild Court.*

A NOTE ON SUSTAINABILITY

RENARD PRESS feels strongly that there is no denying the climate crisis, and we all have a part to play in fixing the problem.

We are proud to be one of the UK's first climate-positive publishers, taking more carbon out of the air than we put in. How? We reduce our emissions as much as possible, using green energy, printing locally and choosing the materials we use carefully; we calculate our carbon footprint and doubly offset it through gold-standard schemes; we replant the trees used to make our books and we plant a tree for every order we receive via our website.

Find out more at:

RENARDPRESS.COM/ECO